Prince Edward Island

Prince Edward Island

Photographs by Wayne Barrett and Edith Robinson

NIMBUS PUBLISHING LIMITED

ACKNOWLEDGEMENTS

We are grateful to many people for their help and encouragement and wish to express our special thanks to Dan Fraser; Catherine Hennessey; Henry Purdy; Neil, Joan, and Linda Robinson; Don Smith; William Toye; and Dr Moncrief Williamson. We are also grateful to the Prince Edward Island Department of Tourism for the use of photographs by Wayne Barrett in their possession and to the Confederation Centre of the Arts for permission to include plate 27.

WB & ER

Canadian Cataloguing in Publication Data

Barrett, Wayne.
Prince Edward Island
ISBN 0-921054-49-1

1. Prince Edward Island — Description and travel — 1951-1980 — Views.*
I. Robinson, Edith. II. Title.

FC2612.B37 1990   971.7′04′0222   C90-097555-5
F1047.8.B37   1990

Printed in Hong Kong by
EVERBEST PRINTING COMPANY LIMITED

We landed that day in four places to see the trees, which are wonderfully beautiful and very fragrant. We discovered that there were cedars, yew-trees, pines, white elms, ash trees, willows and others, many of them unknown to us and all trees without fruit. The soil where there is no trees is also very rich and is covered with peas, white and red gooseberry bushes, strawberries, raspberries, and wild oats like rye, which one would say had been sown there and tilled. It is the best-tempered region one can possibly see and the heat is considerable. There are many turtle-doves, wood-pigeons and other birds. Nothing is wanting but harbours.*

*The description in Jacques Cartier's *Voyages* of his landings on 1 July 1534 as he proceeded from North Cape down the west coast of Prince Edward Island.

Preface

When Edith Robinson and I think about the Island we are glad to be photographers because many of its most enjoyable experiences are visual ones. It is a treasure-trove of scenes and subjects that appeal to us professionally, since we think in images, but that are also part of our lives as Islanders.

The scenes that non-Islanders associate with the Island—rolling green pastures and picturesque villages—are mainly found in the central region, from Summerside to Charlottetown. With its historic Province House, its modern art complex, and many parks, Charlottetown is the heart of the Island, as it should be, for it is the capital. Between Charlottetown and East Point—a little more than half a day's drive away—are forests worked by lumbering men, fishing villages, and the whitest sand beaches. From Summerside to North Cape in the west, known for its French-speaking Acadian communities and its red sandstone cliffs, people make their living from fishing and farming.

You can see most of this by car in a day.

Islanders are a self-sufficient, mild-mannered, friendly people, happiest in a family environment and liking small communities better than large ones. They are glad if change comes slowly. They are proud of their Island—what they experience of it today and what they know of its past. Interest in the past has led to the restoration of old buildings in Charlottetown, which prides itself on hosting the meetings in Province House that led to Confederation in 1867; elsewhere support for historical museums has become a community concern. The Island was visited by Jacques Cartier in 1534. It was named Ile-Saint-Jean by the French, who settled a few thousand colonists there in the eighteenth century. (Our Acadian heritage is most noticeable in Tignish, Egmont Bay, and Abrams Village.) It came under British control in 1763 and was called the Island of St John; annexed to Nova Scotia, it was given its own legislature in 1769. Thirty years later it was renamed Prince Edward Island in honour of the Duke of Kent, the future father of Queen Victoria, and became a paradise for farmers, the 'Garden of the Gulf'.

To an Islander, thinking about the Island is always pleasant because the images that come to mind are good ones:

the early-morning mist rising off water and fields

fishermen leaving Rustico harbour at 5 a.m.

the sweet smell of red clay during the spring thaw

colts frolicking on new pasture grass

the patterns formed by the moving headlights of tractors as they finish their planting or harvesting in darkness

the first strike of sea trout on the Bonshaw River

the first blue heron of the year

the sound of the surf after a storm

church suppers

digging for clams and steaming them over a fire at night

the magnificent sunsets off Cavendish Beach

opening night at Confederation Centre

the checkerboard appearance of the island from the air

Islanders feel sorry for people who can't experience these things as part of their everyday lives. But they like to see visitors enjoy them too. It is in this spirit of sharing a place we love that Edith Robinson and I offer the following selection of our photographs.

WAYNE BARRETT

1 Campbell's Pond Road WB

2 Bonshaw Hills, St Catherines ER

3 New Glasgow WB

4 Loading hay the old way, East Royalty WB

5 Flat River WB

6 Early morning near Winslow WB

7 (right) Boat sailing out
of Rustico harbour at 6 a.m. WB

8 Aerial view, Irish town to North Shore WB

9   The North Shore
Road at Brackley Beach WB

11 Rustico harbour ER

12 Cavendish Beach WB

13 Fishermen's shacks at Covehead ER

14   Sand corrugations left by the tide and waves   ER

15   The end of a
storm, Cable Head Beach   WB

16 Sand patterns WB

17 Breakers on the North Shore ER

18 (left) Sandstone cliffs
sculptured by wind and sea,
Norway ER

19 Lifeguard's hut, Stanhope WB

20 Entering a North Shore harbour ER

21 Johnny Williams,
Beach Point boatbuilder WB

22 View of Charlottetown from Keppoch WB

23 *(right)* Queen Street and harbour, Charlottetown WB

24 Interior of St Dunstan's Basilica, Charlottetown WB

25 (right) Library, theatre, and art gallery in the Confederation Centre of the Arts, Charlottetown, opened in 1964. WB

26 Confederation
Square, Charlottetown WB

27 (right) Some of the cast of *Anne of Green Gables*. This musical by Norman Campbell and Don Harron, based on the novel by L. M. Montgomery, is performed annually in the Charlottetown Summer Festival. 1976. WB

28 *(left)* Beaconsfield, Charlottetown. Designed by William C.
Harris and built in 1877, it is now the home of the Heritage Foundation. ER

29 Government House, Charlottetown. Completed
before 1834, it is the home of the Lieutenant-Governor. ER

30 Province House, Charlottetown (built in 1843-7), with the Confederation Centre in the background. /B

31   Confederation Chamber, Province House. Scene of the Charlottetown
Conference, September 1864, which paved the way for Confederation. WB

32 St Paul's Church, Charlottetown. ER

33 *(right)* House on Water Street,
Charlottetown, built in 1863 ER

34 (left) New Glasgow in the early morning WB

35 Charlottetown in the evening from across the harbour ER

36 A Lady Slipper, floral
emblem of the island ER

37 Campbell's Pond, New Glasgow WB

38 Fishing pond at
Hunter River, early morning WB

39 (*right*) Near Granville WB

40   Scene on St Peter's Road   ER

41 New Glasgow WB

42 Back of Green Road in the fall WB

43 (*right*) MacPhail's Park ER

44 Rusticoville WB

46 *(left)* Potato planting, Tryon ER

47 Potato field, French River WB

48 *(left)* Potato harvesting in the Bedeque area ER

49 Potato plants in blossom ER

50 *(left)* Near New Glasgow ER

51 Farm near Hopedale WB

52 Daybreak WB

53 *(right)* Wharf at Victoria WB

54 Gathering Irish
moss in the National Park ER

55 (right) Rustico ER

DEEP SEA FISHING

COURT BROS

DEEP SEA FISHING
Court Brothers
Phone 9632822 Rustico Harbour
CLOSED EVERY SUNDAY

VISITORS WELCOME
on Fishing Wharf

PARKING

BILL'S TUNA
FISHING

LOBSTER
SUPPERS
Featuring HOME COOKING
DAILY
SERVING FROM 4:00 – 8:30 P.M.
AT THE RECREATION CENTRE
New Glasgow P.E.I

NORTH RUSTICO
MOTEL IN and
COTTAGES

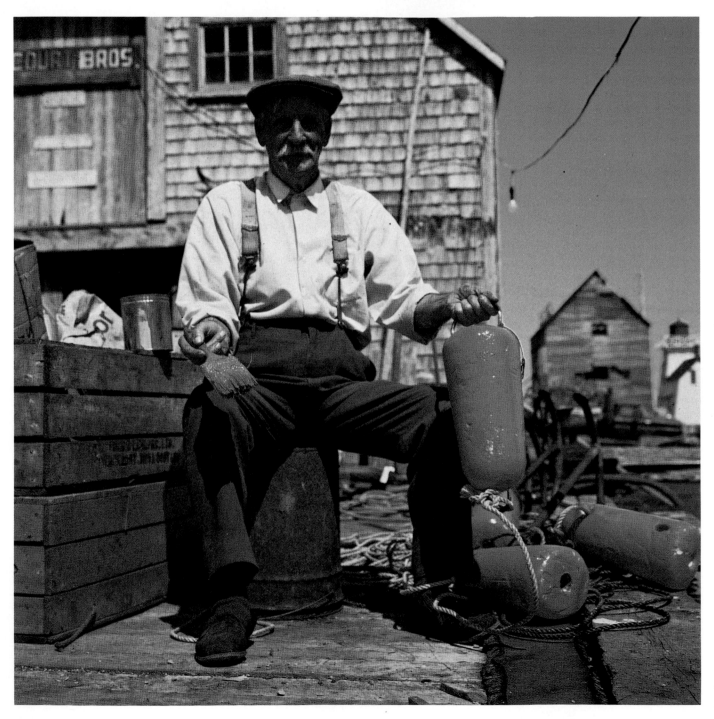

56 Beecher Court
painting buoys, Rustico WB

57 Verde Court, Rustico WB

58 Beecher Court preparing mackerel to be salted ER

59 Queen crabs ER

60 Tuna catch, North Lake WB

61 (*right*) Marina at Summerside WB

62 (*left*) Lambs in early spring ER

63 North Winslow WB

64   *(left)* Christmas trees prepared for
market with boat on stocks, St Peter's WB

65   Farm near Wiltshire WB

66 Near Tryon ER

67   Aerial view of Geddie Memorial Church   WB

68 *(left)* Weeding at West River WB

69 Early morning, Mayfield WB

70 *(left)* Butter factory at
New Glasgow, early morning WB

71 Margate WB

72 Late afternoon
play in the sand dunes WB